Your Baby Boy

A collection by
BARTY PHILLIPS

PIATKUS

Extract from *A Pattern of Islands* by Arthur Grimble on page 50 is reproduced courtesy of the author and John Murray (Publishers) Limited. Excerpt from Maya Angelou's *I Know Why The Caged Bird Sings* on page 4 is courtesy of the author and Virago Press.

First published in Great Britain in 1987 by
Judy Piatkus (Publishers) Limited
5 Windmill Street, London W1P 1HF

British Library Cataloguing in Publication Data

Phillips, Barty
Your baby boy.
1. Infants
I. Title
305.2'32   HQ774

ISBN 0-86188-574-0

Drawings by Paul Saunders
Designed by Sue Ryall
Cover artwork by Sue Warne

Phototypeset in 9/11 pt Linotron Melior
Printed and bound at The Bath Press, Avon

CONTENTS

LULLABIES

I'll buy you a tartan bonnet,
And feathers to put on it,
With a hush-a-bye and a lullaby,
Because you are so like your daddy.

Bye, baby bunting,
Daddy's gone a-hunting,
Gone to get a rabbit skin
To wrap the baby bunting in.

HUSH MY LITTLE BABE!

Hush, hush my little babe!
And thou shalt have in a trice,
Alexandria for thy Sugar
And Cairo for thy rice.

The great Constantinople,
For three long years of pleasure,
Three Asiatic cities,
To fill thy chest with treasure.

Three provinces around,
Their tribute duly bringing,
Three mountain monasteries
With three tall belfries ringing.

A NEW SON

'After a short labor, and without too much pain (I decided that the pain of delivery was overrated), my son was born. Just as gratefulness was confused in my mind with love, so possession became mixed up with motherhood. I had a baby. He was beautiful and mine. Totally mine. No one had bought him for me. No one had helped me endure the sickly gray months. I had had help in the child's conception, but no one could deny that I had had an immaculate pregnancy.

Totally my possession, and I was afraid to touch him. Home from the hospital, I sat for hours by his bassinet and absorbed his mysterious perfection. His extremities were so dainty they appeared unfinished. Mother handled him easily with the casual confidence of a baby nurse, but I dreaded being forced to change his diapers.

Wasn't I famous for awkwardness? Suppose I let him slip, or put my fingers on that throbbing pulse on the top of his head?

Mother came to my bed one night bringing my three-week-old baby. She pulled the cover back and told me to get up and hold him while she put rubber sheets on my bed. She explained that he was going to sleep with me. I begged in vain. I was sure to roll over and crush out his life or break those fragile bones. She wouldn't hear of it, and within minutes the pretty golden baby was lying on his back in the center of my bed, laughing at me.

I lay on the edge of the bed, stiff with fear, and vowed not to sleep all night long. But the eat-sleep routine I had begun in the hospital, and kept up under Mother's dictatorial command, got the better of me. I dropped off.

My shoulder was shaken gently. Mother whispered, "Maya wake up. But don't move." I knew immediately that the awakening had to do with the baby. I tensed. "I'm awake."

She turned the light on and said, "Look at the baby." I didn't hear sadness in her voice, and that helped me to break the bonds of terror. The baby was no longer in the center of the bed. At first I thought he had moved. But after closer investigation I found that I was lying on my stomach with my arm bent at a right angle. Under the tent of blanket, which was poled by my elbow and forearm, the baby slept touching my side.

Mother whispered, "See, you don't have to think about doing the right thing. If you're for the right thing, then you do it without thinking."

She turned out the light and I patted my son's body lightly and went back to sleep.'

(Maya Angelou, from *I Know Why the Caged Bird Sings*)

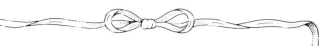

BIRTH CEREMONIES

When a child is born, a community may concentrate
on ceremonies which ward off evil (as in so many
fairy tales such as Sleeping Beauty) or those which
receive the child into the community, as in
Christianity and other religions.

Primitive people often feel afraid of a magical
unluckiness, so before birth they may make women
taboo and isolate them in special huts. Sometimes
there is a ceremony after birth of readmission to the
tribe after the time of seclusion. Hopi Indian women
are not allowed to go out until five days after the birth
and in England there is a custom that the mother
should not go outside afterwards until she has been
'churched'.

These taboos may apply to husbands too. In some
places neither the husband nor the wife is allowed to
approach a fire, eat fruit, bore holes or dive into water
in case they injure the child. In South America, China
and the Pacific Islands the father is put to bed when
the baby is born, sometimes dressed as a woman as if
he had had the baby. He may stay there for days or
even weeks.

In Ancient Greece the father used to run round the
hearth after the birth; in Estonia he ran round the
church while the baby was being baptised. In parts of
the Philippines the husband stands on the house
brandishing a sword. Amulets and charms are often

fastened to the new born to protect it from evil. A Navaho Indian child's life is marked by rituals. A flint is used to cut the umbilical cord and the woman who assists with the birth has the privilege of holding the child first. The baby is laid next to his mother with his head to the north and annointed with corn pollen—a symbol of life.

In the folk belief of nearly all the peoples of the world, the afterbirth is closely associated with the soul, life, death, health, character, success or failure of the child. What becomes of it determines the child's life. Some Indian tribes present a boy's afterbirth to the ravens so that he will see into the future. The Aymora Indians of Bolivia cover the afterbirth with flowers and bury it with tiny farm tools if it's a boy. In Java the women place the afterbirth in a little vessel, bedeck it with fruits, flowers and lighted candles and set it adrift in the river at night to appease the crocodiles (who are supposed to be inhabited by the ancestors of these people).

Among certain tribes of Central Africa, the afterbirth is considered to be the actual twin of the child and is put in a pot and buried under a plantain tree, for that is where the ghost (or twin) lives. If anyone not related makes food or drink from this tree, the ghost will depart and the child will follow its twin and die.

MY LITTLE SON

My little son, I wish you well, your mother's
    comfort when in grief
My pretty boy what can I do? Will you not give
    one hour's relief?
Sleep has just past, and me he asked if this my
    son in slumber lay.
Close, close your little eyes my child; send your
    sweet breath far leagues away.
You are the fount of rose water; you are with
    every beauty fraught
Sleep, darling son, my pretty one, my golden
    button richly wrought.

A Sicilian lullaby

HISTORY OF BABY BOYS

In historic times, girls were cherished and praised and enjoyed a freedom unthinkable in later times, but in classical history boys have been prized and girls put up with—and sometimes not even that. In ancient Greece the aim of marriage was to produce a son and heir. Not too many, however, because that would split the wealth of a family. 'May you have no more than a single son to keep the patrimony together. That is the way to preserve wealth' said Hesiod, one of the earliest of the ancient Greek poets, who lived a little later than Homer. 'Even a poor man will bring up a son, but even a rich man will expose a daughter' said another Greek poet.

If girls were exposed to die, boys were often exposed to make them tough. And no doubt this practice of leaving babies exposed to the elements accounts for many of the stories of babies being found and brought up by wild animals such as wolves or bears. In Sparta all citizens were trained for war from boyhood and baby boys learned to be tough from the moment they were born. Spartans became proverbial for their indifference to pain or death and their contempt for luxury and the arts—hence the word 'spartan'.

Scotland was another warlike country where boy babies were often exposed to rough weather in the mists and mountains of the highlands and the border

country to toughen them up and prepare them for clan feuds and battles with England.

Royal babies found floating down rivers in woven rush baskets were often put there by their anxious mothers or nurses to save them from the wrath of jealous fathers or stepfathers who saw them as a threat to future ambitions and possible usurpers of their power.

The life expectancy of any baby up until the eighteenth century was pretty small. Parents didn't allow themselves to become overfond of their babies since they were so likely to die. This is one reason why it was an accepted custom to allow babies to be adopted by a wet nurse. A household manual called *The Nurse's Guide*, put down the Roman emperor Caligula's drunkenness to vices drawn in with the milk from his wet nurse.

Among the most miserable babies in history must have been the sons of the Turkish Sultans, born in the harem. These poor little princes, often several hundred at a time, were cooped up in a two-storied building known as 'the cage'. This was situated right in the middle of the Seraglio, surrounded by a high and dismal wall. There, they received no education, were brought no news of the outside world, had no one to talk to or learn from as their only companions were deaf mutes and 'sterile women'. It's hardly surprising that the one or two who survived to be Sultans over the centuries were self indulgent, half mad and themselves excessively cruel.

In ancient times when the expectation of life was much shorter, boys (and girls too) were expected to play an adult's role at an age when we would still think of them as children. Juliet was only thirteen when she fell in love with Romeo, and Romulus Augustus, the last Roman emperor in the West, was made emperor by his soldier father Orestes when he was fourteen.

Both sons and daughters are celebrated in Japan where there is a separate festival for each. The boys' festival is called *Tango No Sekku* and takes place on May 5. The festival is celebrated by families who have boys under the age of seven. In each home the family sets up a display of dolls dressed as ancient warriors and surrounded by a collection of miniature weapons.

In nearly all societies today it is still considered 'manly' to play at war; boys are still encouraged to play with weapons and to act out battles. Only very recently have men been expected (or prepared) to take part, or even take an interest in caring for their own babies. The now fairly common sight of men wheeling prams or changing nappies or being present at the birth of their children is still very new.

NINNA AND ANNINIA

Oh! ninna and anninia!
  Sleep, baby boy;
Oh! ninna and anninia!
  God give thee joy.
Oh! ninna and anninia!
  Sweet joy be thine;
Oh! ninna and anninia!
  Sleep, brother mine.

Sleep and do not cry,
  Pretty, pretty one,
Apple of my eye,
  Danger there is none;
Sleep, for I am by,
  Mother's darling son.

Oh! ninna and anninia!
  Sleep, baby boy;
Oh! ninna and anninia!
  God give thee joy.
Oh! ninna and anninia!
  Sweet joy be thine;
Oh! ninna and anninia!
  Sleep, brother mine.

Sardinian lullaby

FAMOUS BABIES
IN MYTH AND HISTORY

There are several babies in myth who were abandoned or lost and brought up by wolves. One of these is an ancient Irish story about Conn of the Hundred Battles, contained in the *Book of Ballymore* which goes like this: When Art, son of Conn, travelled west to fight the battle of May Mucrama, he spent the eve of the battle in the house of a smith and 'begot a son on the smith's daughter Erain.'

Art told Erain that her son would be king of Ireland. She was to bring him to be fostered by a woman called Lugna Fer Tri. Art was killed in the battle; Erain set out to the foster home before the child's birth but labour pains overtook her on the way and she gave birth in a bed of ferns. A clap of thunder (at the moment of the boy's birth) announced to Lugna that Cormac, son of Art, was in the world. Lugna set out to find him. But while Erain and her maid slept, wolves carried Cormac away.

However, someone reported to Lugna that a child had been seen crawling among some wolf whelps. The child and the whelps were taken and brought up with Lugna's sons. Eventually, sure enough, Cormac became king and, loyal to his first family, always kept his wolves with him.

★

Rudyard Kipling's Mowgli, abandoned in the jungle, was found by a she-wolf and brought up as a member of the wolf pack, learned the law of the jungle and became friends with the snake, the jaguar and the bear.

★

The most famous baby to be brought up by wolves was probably Romulus, legendary founder and first king of Rome. He was the son of the war god Mars and was exposed with his twin brother Remus, by their great uncle Anulius. But they were suckled by a she-wolf and rescued by a shepherd. When they grew to manhood they killed Anulius and founded Rome. Romulus, however, murdered Remus and ruled alone until he disappeared in a storm and thereafter was worshipped as a god under the name of Quirinus.

DUTCH LULLABY

Wynken, Blynken and Nod, one night
Sailed off in a wooden shoe—
Sailed on a river of silvery light
Into a sea of dew:
'Where are you going and what do you wish?'
The old moon asked the three;—
'We have come to fish for the herring fish
That live in this beautiful sea;
Nets of silver and gold have we!'
   said Wynken,
        Blynken
        And Nod.

The old man laughed and sang a song,
As they rocked in the wooden shoe,
And the wind that sped them all night long
Ruffled the waves of dew.
The little stars were the herring fish
That lived in that beautiful sea;—
'Now cast your nets wherever you wish—
Never afeared are we;'
So cried the stars to the fishermen three;
   Wynken,
   Blynken
   And Nod.

All night long their nets they threw
To the stars in the twinkling foam—
Then down from the skies came the wooden shoe
Bringing the fishermen home;
T'was all so pretty a sail, it seemed
As if it could not be,
And some folks thought 'twas a dream they'd dreamed
Of sailing that beautiful sea;—
But I shall name you the fishermen three;
    Wynken,
    Blynken
    And Nod.

Wynken and Blynken are two little eyes,
And Nod is a little head,
And the wooden shoe that sailed the skies
Is a wee one's truckle bed.
So shut your eyes while mother sings
Of wonderful sights that be,
And you shall see the beautiful things,
As you rock in the misty sea
Where the old shoe rocked the fishermen three;
    Wynken,
    Blynken
    And Nod.

STAR SIGNS

The sun passes through one of the twelve signs of the Zodiac each month. The simplest horoscopes are based on the position of the sun when a baby is born without taking the other planets into account. It is a rough and ready way of assessing character but often surprisingly accurate.

If the birthday falls in the middle of the Zodiacal period the baby will have strong characteristics of his or her sign. If it falls on either side, he or she will incorporate some of those belonging to the neighbouring sign.

The signs fall into four categories: Earth people are generally practical, Air people thoughtful, Fire people idealistic and Water people emotional.

21 March–20 April:  **ARIES THE RAM**

Fire sign. Colour, red. Aries is the symbol of spring. These people are pioneers in thought and action, brave, adventurous and fond of travel, though highly strung with a tendency to head and toothaches. Your child will be ambitious, self reliant, energetic and impulsive and will be walking almost before crawling. He will be loyal if treated well, act impulsively if dissatisfied. Full of schemes and ideas but has the urge to do things quickly. Anything needing patience or dedication will soon be

abandoned. Your baby will love to talk and may
embroider on the truth just for fun. Arians often
become designers, architects, writers or entertainers.
Famous Arians include Pearl Bailey, Alec Guinness,
Charlie Chaplin. Compatible signs are other Arians,
Leos and Sagittarians.

21 April–21 May: TAURUS THE BULL

Earth sign. Colours, blue and pink. Taureans are
pretty healthy on the whole: inclined to chest and
throat ailments if anything. They often have good
singing voices. Taurus indicates strength of character
and purpose and a Taurus baby may be led but never
driven and determined to the point of obstinacy. Such
children need security, are slow to anger but have
violent tempers when roused, though they are usually
quick to forgive. They make good organisers and
managers and are financially astute. Famous Taureans
include Catharine the Great, Salvador Dali.
Compatible signs are other Taureans, Capricorn and
Virgo.

22 May–21 June: GEMINI THE TWINS

An Air sign. Colour, bright yellow. Gemini indicates a
contradictory nature which makes such children
elusive and rather unpredictable but they are very
affectionate. They are adaptable and versatile and
need constant variety. They seldom lose control and

cope well in emergencies but find it difficult to concentrate on one thing for any length of time, whether a project or a person. Famous Geminis include Judy Garland, Queen Victoria, Paul McCartney. Compatible signs are other Geminis, Aquarians and Librans.

22 June–22 July:  CANCER THE CRAB

Water sign. Colour, violet. Cancerians respond to the changing influence of the moon but are also tenacious and obstinate. They are deeply moved by the fortunes of other people. They are conservative and home loving, liable to have romantic ideals. Such babies will be inventive and original, excellent mimics with good memories. They often surprise their families by being shy and possessive. They love comfort and good living which makes them grow up to become good cooks and homekeepers. Eventually your child will probably veer towards the arts and will want to travel. Famous Cancerians include Gina Lollobrigida, Rembrandt. Compatible signs are other Cancerians, Pisces, Scorpios.

23 July–23 August: LEO THE LION

Fire sign. Colour, orange. Proud, ambitious, masterful, sincere and generous, Leo is the king of signs. Leos love everything big in life, are trusting and good hearted, practical and hard headed, with plenty of will-power and self control. Do not be surprised if

your child sets high goals for him or herself,
particularly in controlling others rather than in
manual skills. Typical careers might be as an
orchestra conductor, organist, actor, mural
painter—anything grand. Famous Leos include
Princess Anne and Napoleon. Compatible signs are
other Leos, Aries and Sagittarius.

24 August–23 September: VIRGO THE VIRGIN

Earth sign. Colours, grey or navy. You can often tell
Virgos by their rather prominent, aquiline noses.
Your baby will grow up to have an analytical mind
but a matter of fact front may hide a nervous nature.
Virgos may not show what they are feeling but
nevertheless feel very strongly.

They are rather exacting to people they are close to
though always just in what they expect. They are
shrewd and inventive with words, methodical and
logical with a good eye for detail. They are also
practical with their hands and make good
technicians. Famous Virgoans include Elizabeth I, Dr.
Johnson and D. H. Lawrence. Your baby will make
friends with other Virgoans, Capricorns and Taureans.

24 September–23 October: LIBRA THE BALANCE

Air sign. Colour, indigo. Librans are charming, fun
loving and appreciate beauty, elegance and harmony.
They are impartial and fair, great observers, curious

about people. Take care, your baby will listen carefully and pick up and take in everything you say including social gossip. The Libran's impartiality leads them to be arrogant in the belief that they can't be wrong and they often refuse to enter into arguments or discussions and absolutely hate quarrels. Famous Librans include Lady Jane Grey, Mahatma Ghandi. Compatible signs are other Librans, Aquarians and Geminis.

24 October–22 November: SCORPIO THE SCORPION

Water sign. Colour, deep red. This sign indicates a smooth surface with hidden depths. These people have very powerful natures, are calm and watchful but with magnetic intensity and can have a hypnotic influence over people. Your baby will be strong willed, determined, yet cautious, shrewd and self confident; will be very direct in giving opinions and sometimes quick to take offence. Nevertheless Scorpios make good friends, possessive and passionate lovers. They often become public speakers, detectives or doctors. Famous Scorpios include Katharine Hepburn, Mary Queen of Scots, Prince Charles. Compatible signs are other Scorpios, Pisces and Cancer.

23 November–21 December:  SAGITTARIUS THE ARCHER

Fire sign. Colour, light blue. Sagittarians are honest, optimistic, trustworthy and loyal but very independent and tend to be restless. Your baby will feel cramped by a play pen and will want to be exploring the world. They are natural teachers and philosophers though inclined to be outspoken and impulsive. They may be attracted to politics, teaching, law or religion. Famous Sagittarians include Jane Austen, Winston Churchill. Compatible signs are other Sagittarians, Arians and Leos.

22 December–20 January: 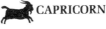 CAPRICORN THE GOAT

Earth sign. Colour, green. Capricorn people are economical, practical, perservering, shrewd and diplomatic, though likely to rush into things and sometimes behave unexpectedly. Your baby will enjoy learning and arguing, will grow to enjoy being in authority in any chosen profession and will be a loyal friend and lover, though may decide to live alone. Other famous Capricorns include Joan of Arc and Mozart. Their most compatible signs are other Capricorns, Taureans and Virgos.

21 January–19 February:  AQUARIUS THE WATER CARRIER

Air sign. Colour, bright blue. Your Aquarian will have an open, outgoing personality and an inquiring mind. Such children may have unexpected outbursts of temper, throwing their toys across the room in a fit of rage but at other times they are gregarious and fun loving. They have rather contradictory natures, being both idealistic and practical. They will have strong maternal instincts and love teaching. They are faithful and loving but expect a great deal of others. Interests are likely to be poetry, astronomy, music and entertainment. Famous Aquarians include Dame Edith Evans, Charles Dickens. Compatible signs are other Aquarians, Geminis and Librans.

20 February–20 March: PISCES THE FISH

Water sign. Colour, sea green. At their best they are good natured, friendly and kind. Your baby will be quick to learn, have a vivid imagination, be interested in music and the arts, the mysterious and literature. He or she may lose confidence from time to time and need special comforting. Pisces people don't find it easy to concentrate and many follow two or more interests at once. Typical careers are as nurses, librarians or designers. Famous Pisceans include Elizabeth Taylor, Hans Christian Andersen. Compatible signs are other Pisces, Cancer and Scorpio.

BIRTH STONES

Particular precious or semi-precious stones and particular flowers are supposed to bring luck to those born at certain times of year. Lucky stones for birth months are said to be:

JANUARY—Garnet (*constancy*): a semi-precious stone usually red, looking a bit like a ruby. It is said to make the wearer cheerful.

FEBRUARY—Amethyst (*sincerity*): a kind of quartz coloured purple or violet. In Greek it means to protect from being drunk. Lucky to lovers.

MARCH—Bloodstone (*courage*): a dark green semi-precious stone with red spots like small bloodstains. Soldiers used to wear it thinking it would staunch wounds.

APRIL—Diamond (*purity*): diamonds are water coloured and brilliantly sparkling. They should be worn on the left side and symbolise strength, virtue, courage and insight.

MAY—Emerald (*hope*): a beautiful green stone. The Romans believed it was good for the eyes which is why the Emperor Nero wore emerald eyeglasses.

JUNE—Agate (*health*): a semi-precious stone with stripes of colour usually brown, dark red or yellow,

but sometimes blue or green. Lucky for foresters, farmers and gardeners. Good for friendship.

JULY—Ruby (*contentment*): a precious jewel similar to sapphire except in colour which can be deep glowing red or pink to almost violet. Assuages grief, brings good friendships.

AUGUST—Sardonyx (*fidelity*): a handsome stone, a type of onyx with white and dark red or dark brown markings in bands. Said to bring married happiness and protect from snake bites.

SEPTEMBER—Sapphire (*repentance*): a precious stone which at its best is a clear cornflower blue. Lucky to lovers; brings peace and optimism.

OCTOBER—Opal (*lovableness*): a cloudy white stone with hidden rainbow colours when it catches the light. Known as the stone of tears because it is brittle and inclined to break. Gives second sight, hope and faith to those whose birth stone it is.

NOVEMBER—Topaz (*cheerfulness*): a more or less transparent precious stone usually of a clear yellow, though sometimes yellowish white, blue or pink. Supposed to ward off bronchitis and asthma and bring friendship and love.

DECEMBER—Turquoise (*unselfishness*): a sea blue, opaque precious stone whose colour and sheen vary depending on the mood of the wearer. Protects from danger and sorrow.

BIRTH FLOWERS

January—carnations and snowdrops
February—primroses
March—daffodils
April—daisies
May—lilies of the valley
June—roses
July—water lilies
August—gladioli
September—asters
October—dahlias
November—chrysanthemums
December—holly

LULLABY OF
AN INFANT CHIEF

O hush thee, my babie thy sire was a knight,
Thy mother a lady, both lovely and bright;
The woods and the glens, from the towers which
   we see,
They all are belonging, dear babie to thee.
O ho ro, i ri ri, cadul gu lo,
O ho ro, i ri ri, cadul gu lo.

O, fear not the bugle, though loudly it blows,
It calls but the warders that guard thy repose;
Their bows would be bended, their blades
   would be red,
Ere the step of a foreman draws near to thy bed.
O ho ro, i ri ri etc.

O, hush thee, my babie, the time will soon come,
When thy sleep will be broken by trumpet and drum;
Then hush thee, my darling, take a rest while
   you may,
For strife comes with manhood, and waking
   with day.
O ho ri, i ri ri, etc.

Sir Walter Scott

FOR A HEALTHY BOY

The tree of life or the 'birth tree' has an important significance in many cultures to the health of a child. If you plant a tree for the baby it will watch over his health all his life. If it thrives, so will the child, if it withers or is felled, the child will become sick or die or be injured. This is still a common belief in Europe, especially in Germany. In Switzerland the tree should specifically be an apple tree for boys and a pear tree for girls. The birth tree is still a living practice among the Papuans, the Dayaks of Borneo, the Balinese, and the Maoris of New Zealand, in various parts of Africa and certain North American Indians. The tree of life is a motif of many folk tales in England, France, Germany, Italy, Eastern European countries and Russia and is often used in embroidery motifs in those countries. Sometimes a fully grown tree is acclaimed as the child's tree at birth and the afterbirth and umbilical cord are buried beneath it.

Culpeper, author of the famous Herbal, had plenty of advice on herbal remedies for children. 'Fennel leaves or seed boiled in barley water and drank are good for nurses to increase their milk and make it more wholesome for the child: the leaves or rather the seeds, boiled in water, stayeth the hiccough ...

'Lettuce also increaseth the milk in nurses and mallow or marshmallow roots boiled in wine and water used by nurses procureth them stores of milk.'

On the other hand, ointment made from the poplar tree was much used to dry up the milk in women's breasts when they had weaned their children.

Culpeper also quotes the Ancient Greek physician Galen who wrote 500 treatises on medicine: he 'saith that the roots and leaves of the cotton thistle will help to prevent rickets in children; purslaine juice is used with oil of roses' applied to the navels of children that stick forth, it helpeth them. It is also good for sore mouths and gums that are swollen.'

★

Beatrix Potter's Mrs. Rabbit, that most motherly of mothers, felt it necessary to send Peter Rabbit to bed early with a dose of chamomile tea when he returned from his escapade in Mr. McGregor's garden.

Meanwhile, she and the good girl rabbits stayed up and ate blackberries.

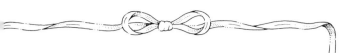

MONDAY'S CHILD ...

Monday's child is fair of face,
Tuesday's child is full of grace,
Wednesday's child is full of woe,
Thursday's child has far to go,
Friday's child is loving and giving,
Saturday's child works hard for a living,
But the child that is born on the Sabbath day
Is bonny and blythe and good and gay.

BIRTHMARKS AND
SUPERSTITIONS

Giving birth has become a much safer process than in the past and it is no longer necessary to invoke magic spells to ensure a safe birth and a healthy baby. But some superstitions still persist. Babies born early through some form of caesarian operation were thought to be magical or special. For instance MacDuff who was 'from his mother's womb untimely ripped' was able to vanquish MacBeth. It used to be widely believed (and in some countries still is) that a birthmark was the result of the mother having seen something unpleasant while she was pregnant, or even that she had been touched by some demon or other evil spirit during her pregnancy. Mothers were supposed to lick the mark for several days after the child was born, and indeed, spittle does seem to have had curative powers in some cases.

Birthmarks or strawberry marks were often useful as a proof that a baby was of royal blood, since the birthmark was often hereditary. On some Greek Islands such marks are known as 'the fating' or 'the fates'.

Moles are often signs of good luck, for instance a mole in the middle of the forehead or between the wrist and the elbow means money later on, while one just above the temple implies a person of wit and understanding. Moles on the chin, ear and neck, are lucky and the girl with a mole on her left breast will

be irresistible to men. There are many other lucky omens: a German superstition says that if clouds are shaped like flocks of sheep or lambs at the time of birth the baby will be lucky and in Yorkshire they say the baby should be carried to the top of the house so that it will 'rise in the world'. In some places it is the custom to show a child two objects (a violin and a purse, say) and the one it reaches for will indicate its future occupation.

Parents can take heart that 'a child who cries long will live long'; a child born feet first (a 'footling') will have the power to cure muscular pains and become a local healer. A bald baby will grow up to be a brilliant scholar, but a child weaned in Spring will become prematurely grey haired and a child born with teeth will be selfish (biting the breast that feeds it, no doubt).

Seven has always been a lucky number. 'Seventh son of seventh son, will be nature's lucky one': He can cure disease, has second sight and can tell the future. Simply to be a seventh child is lucky and if the birth date is divisible by seven the child will be lucky.

Seven could obviously be lucky for the parent too as this Danish nursery rhyme shows:

> Adam he had seven sons
> Seven sons had Adam;
> Seven sons who always did
> Exactly what he bade 'em.
> So Adam, you may well believe,
> Was very glad he'd had 'em.

GRANDMOTHERS' HINTS ON BRINGING UP LITTLE BOYS

'Spare the rod and spoil the child' was a phrase often used by the Victorians to justify punishing children. Boys in particular were felt in need of punishment because they were inherently naughty. Caning and 'slippering' were notoriously common in English public schools, and in Scotland until 1982 the tawse was frequently used to hit children's hands when they misbehaved or failed to answer questions in class.

Little boys were sent away to boarding school at the age of seven or perhaps even five, to learn to become leaders of men. They were discouraged from crying or 'blubbering' which was considered 'cissy' and babyish. 'Put a brave face on it'; 'keep a stiff upper lip'; 'pull your socks up'; 'soldier on'; 'pull yourself together' were all phrases little boys became familiar with at home and at school. In fact they were expected to obey orders and show no emotion like miniature soldiers. Indeed many of them would inevitably grow up to become officers in the army where no doubt all their early training stood them in good stead.

Another trying part of growing up for young boys was the keeping of Sunday. This was particularly strictly kept in Scotland where you were not allowed to play games on the Sabbath and children might well have to attend church twice on that day as well as going to Sunday School. As late as 1940 one small

Scots child who asked his aunt if he could read a
book was told: 'Well, I suppose so, just as long as you
don't enjoy it.'

★

The Duchess in Lewis Carroll's *Alice in Wonderland*
had if anything even stricter views on children's
behaviour. When Alice first came across her in the
kitchen of a large house, 'The Duchess was sitting on a
three-legged stool nursing a baby; the cook was
leaning over the fire, stirring a large cauldron which
seemed full of soup. "There's certainly too much
pepper in that soup" Alice said to herself, as well as
she could for sneezing.

There was certainly too much of it in the air. Even
the Duchess sneezed occasionally and the baby was
sneezing and howling alternatively without a
moment's pause ... The Duchess began nursing the
child again, singing as she did so and giving it a
violent shake at the end of every line.

> "Speak roughly to your little boy,
> And beat him when he sneezes;
> He only does it to annoy,
> Because he knows it teases."

CHORUS (in which the cook and the baby joined)
"Wow! Wow! Wow!."

While the Duchess sang the second verse of the song
she kept tossing the baby violently up and down and

the poor little thing howled so that Alice could hardly hear the words:

> "I speak severely to my boy,
> I beat him when he sneezes;
> For he can thoroughly enjoy
> The pepper when he pleases!"
> CHORUS: "Wow! Wow! Wow!"'

Amidst all this punishing was nevertheless a wish to bring children up to be 'chivalrous' which, since the Crusades and before had been considered another necessary manly virtue. Chivalry meant treating gentlewomen like china shepherdesses. Even a 1920s book on home management suggested that the furnishings of the nursery should include a cuckoo clock and 'a weather box from which the "little man" emerges in wet weather to impart the earliest lesson in chivalry'.

LAVENDER'S BLUE

Lavender's Blue dilly dilly,
Lavender's Green
When I am king, dilly, dilly,
You shall be queen.

Call up your men dilly dilly,
Set them to work,
Some to the plough, dilly dilly,
Some to the fork.

Some to make hay dilly, dilly,
Some to cut corn,
Whilst you and I, dilly dilly,
Keep ourselves warm.

Roses are red, dilly dilly,
Violets are blue,
Because you love me, dilly, dilly,
I will love you.

Let the birds sing, dilly, dilly
And let the lamb's play,
We shall be safe dilly, dilly,
Out of harm's way.

HISTORY OF BABY CLOTHES

During the Middle Ages very young children wore long dresses or gowns, and there was no distinction between boys and girls. A traditional infant's gown or christening robe is at least twice as long as the baby. In 1575 the granddaughter of the Earl of Bedford wore 'a mantell of crimson velvet garded with two wrought laces having also over the face a lawne striped with bone of lace of gold overthwart and striped with gold flowers and white wrought thereon.'

Between the ages of three and six boys became mini men and girls mini women as far as dress was concerned, and of course this restricted their potential for playing, since there was no freedom of movement. Ruffs, farthingales, padded breeches, trailing sleeves, dragging skirts, high heeled shoes and hats all prevented children from behaving like children.

By the later half of the eighteenth century a more humane understanding of the needs of children began to prevail. Here is a layette suggested for a baby in 1843:

4 night gowns
4 first-sized day caps
5 long robes
4 day gowns for the first month
8 pinafores
2 doz napkins
3 flannel barrows (a long flannel wrapped round under the arms and pinned up over the feet)

9 back wrappers
4 flannel belts or soft calico binders
3 whittles (large white shawls)
6 first sized shirts
2 flannel caps
2 short chemises
baby linen, basket and cover
powder box, pincushion
feather for bed
soft sponge and soft brush for the hair

By the late 1870s little girls were wearing simple,
comfortable, low-necked muslin frocks and boys were
dressed a in short jacket with soft turnover collar and
trousers buttoned onto the jacket. Flat slippers were
the order of the day and simple haircuts for both boys
and girls.

Kate Greenaway, a 1920s illustrator of children's
books, dressed the children in her drawings in
fashions of a hundred years before her time, because
she liked them. People began to copy the idea and put
real children into similar clothes.

Nowadays, happily, baby clothes are governed by
the needs of the baby and the convenience of the
mother and modern fibres and textiles have produced
clothes that are easy to wash, to wear and to play in.

HISTORY OF
THE BABY CARRIAGE

Baby carriages of one sort or another have been used for centuries. In Athens a clay model of a baby cart has been dug up and there is pictorial evidence of their use in fourteenth century India and Ceylon.

Britain seems to have caught on to the idea rather late on, presumably relying on nursery maids until the nineteenth century when wooden baby carriages were made for the very rich. Those built for Lady Georgina Cavendish at Chatsworth were adult coaches in minature and very elaborate. In the 1840s experiments were made with various designs including three wheelers, carriages to be pulled, some to be pushed and the first patent was taken out by Charles Burton in 1853 for 'The Perambulator'. In 1853 he opened a showroom in Oxford Street with four other manufacturers. Queen Victoria bought three Burton carriages.

Early British 'prams' were pretty dangerous, having no springs and arsenic coated harnesses. They also gave an opportunity for nursemaids to neglect their small charges. However, many had considerable grace and beauty, with liveried wooden casings surrounded by miniature balustrades, lined with buttoned leather and trimmed in gleaming brass. Bassinet versions (popular in the USA and colonies) were reed woven in shell-coiled arabesques with parasols or canopies

fluttering overhead to keep off the sun. Eventually simpler two-handled carts were developed, like those which postmen had been using. They were cheaper and lighter, easier to manoeuvre and dashingly designed. Eventually they became upholstered with attachments across the handles to allow babies to lie full length.

By the 1900s baby carriages had become very sophisticated. Double hoods meant that two babies could be housed in all weathers and carriage lanterns on the mudguards allowed the nurse to go for extended walks far into the twilight or fog. Mothers were only very occasionally to be seen wheeling *their own* carriages: 'a crucial test of your moral courage and innate ladyhood' said one mother of the time.

SINGING AND
TALKING GAMES

A parent who talks frequently and closely to a baby
with eye contact and pronounced lip movements will
be much more likely to find the baby talking back and
responding. Singing and talking games are a time
honoured way of encouraging babies to respond and
of helping them to grasp the meanings of words. Such
games are very important as an introduction to
communication. Babies love to have these games
repeated over and over again and that is how they
learn.

There are many rhymes to demonstrate parts of the
body.

For instance here's one for the face:

> Here sits the Lord Mayor (forehead)
> Here sits his men, (eyes)
> Here sits the cockadoodle, (right cheek)
> Here sits the hen, (left cheek)
> Here sit the little chickens, (teeth)
> Here they run in (mouth)
> Chin chopper, chin chopper,
> Chin chopper, chin.

And several for the fingers:

> Thumbikin, Thumbikin broke the barn,
> Pinnikin, Pinnikin, stole the corn,
> Long back'd Gray carried it away,
> Old Mid-man sat and saw,
> But peesy-weesy paid for a'.

>> Thumb he
>> Wizbee
>> Long man
>> Cherry tree
>> Little jack-a-dandy.

>> Little Pig
>> Phillimore
>> Grimthistle
>> Pennywhistle
>> Great Big Thumbo
>> Father of them all.

And a favourite one for the toes:

> This little pig went to market,
> This little pig stayed at home,
> This little pig had roast beef,
> This little pig had none,
> And this little pig cried
> Wee Wee Wee Wee, all the way home.

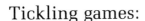

Tickling games:

Round and round the garden [palm of the hand],
Like a Teddy bear;
One step, two step
And tickly under there [the armpit].

Round about, round about, here sits the hare
In the corner of a cornfield and that's just there
    [by the thumb]
This little dog found her
This little dog ran her
This little dog caught her
This little dog ate her
And this little dog said 'Give me a little bit
    please.'

Knee rides and dandling:

Babies still love knee rides of which these are among
the best known:

> Dance to your daddy,
> My little babby,
> Dance to your daddy,
> My little lamb.
>
> You shall have a fishy,
> In a little dishy,
> You shall have a fishy
> When the boat comes in.

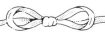

You shall have an apple
You shall have a plum,
You shall have a rattle basket
When your daddy comes home.

In Scotland, there's a slightly different version:

Dance to your daddie,
My bonnie laddie,
Dance to your daddie,
My bonnie lamb.
And ye'll get a coatie,
And a pair of breekies—
Ye'll get a whippie
And a supple tam!

And another great favourite with babies is this:

This is the way the ladies ride,
Trit trot trit trot trit trot trit trot;
This is the way the gentlemen ride
gallopy, gallopy, gallopy, gallopy
This is the way the farmers ride
Trot trot trot trot trot trot trot trot.
This is the way the ploughboys ride
Hobble dee hobble dee hobble dee—and DOWN
into a ditch.

FIRST TOYS

For the first few months what a baby needs most of all is contact with people. Objects are meaningless at this stage. His best 'toys' are listening to his parents' voices and studying their faces and he will love to be picked up and held closely.

From four to five weeks your baby will begin to experience where his body ends and the world begins. He will enjoy watching mobiles, will like the sensation of a warm bath and will begin to take notice of rattles or toys strung across his pram.

From about twelve weeks baby will begin to want to hold things. This is the time when rattles begin to come into their own and when he will begin to discover that he has some control over creating rattling noises. Babies are attracted by bright colours and enjoy learning about shapes so a variety of rattles is a good idea: also woolly balls, plastic bottles with different objects inside to make different sounds (well sealed of course) will all be of interest. Dried peas, paper clips, sand, all make different sounds.

Some babies can swing and jump happily from baby bouncers usually hung from a strong hook in the doorway. If the ceiling is high enough, baby can bounce on the table where he will enjoy being on a level with you.

From about six months babies will have fun playing with household objects, a toothbrush, saucepan and

wooden spoon, own spoon and beaker, toys with
wheels, toys that squeak when squeezed, paper to tear.
An activity centre attached to the cot bars may
encourage him to play quietly early in the morning
before you have woken up.

Balls to roll (marbles are too small and get popped
into small mouths), bricks, toys to experiment with in
terms of texture and behaviour (biscuits crumble,
bread is squashy, apples are smooth and hard). Ping
pong balls can be rolled down a cardboard tube, a
xylophone makes interesting sounds.

At the crawling stage your son will love big
wheeled toys, cushions, enormous Teddy bears, big
balls and will be fascinated by seeing his own face in
a plastic mirror.

THINGS TO MAKE

First baby carriage toy

Babies like brightly coloured objects strung along the front of the pram. For these little balls use five different bright colours of felt and stuff them with kapok or old (but clean) tights cut up small.

Each ball is made of four segments. Draw a line 3 in long and across the middle of it draw a line 1½ in long. Now draw a curve from one long end to the other, touching each end of the short line. Cut out the segment shape in thin card. From this template you can cut as many segments of felt as you need. If you want to embroider the felt, do it now. Join the pieces together using oversewing. Leave the last two sides open. Ease the stuffing in, pressing it into shape. Sew up the opening. Cut two small circles or flower shapes. Punch a hole in the centre of each and Copydex or stitch over the joined points. Thread elastic through, using a bodkin. Five of these strung together will be enough to stretch across the carriage.

First mobile

Babies love to watch things move, lying out of doors they will delight in watching the leaves waving in the breeze and the clouds racing by. A very simple mobile can be made by cutting thick coloured card into simple shapes and hanging them from a wire coat hanger, or hang from it a variety of different small objects; a shiny spoon, a cotton reel, a plastic duck, all at slightly different heights. Place it where he can see it while lying in his cot, but where he can't reach up and grab it as he grows older.

NEW BORN

My mother groan'd! My father wept.
Into the dangerous world I leapt:
Helpless, naked, piping loud:
Like a fiend hid in a cloud.

Struggling in my father's hands,
Striving against my swaddling bands,
Bound and weary I thought best
To sulk upon my mother's breast.

(William Blake, from Songs of Experience)

NAME CEREMONIES

In many societies the baby's name has a spiritual importance and must be chosen with great care. Eskimos say that a person is made up of body, soul and name, the name being the part which survives death.

One common idea is that a baby is an ancestor reborn. The parents must discover the ancestor's name, rather than choose their own name for the baby. This is done by holding the baby up while it is crying and repeating a list of family names. When the baby stops crying—that is its name.

In some places the parents are considered virtually 'impure' for ten days after the birth and are kept in isolation. On the tenth day the child is given a public name and the impurity of the parents is ended.

There is often a fixed date after the birth for the name giving ceremony. In ancient Greece it is the tenth day. In South Germany it was thought that the soul flew about between rebirths in the form of a butterfly. In China a new born babe is presented before the gods and communion established between it and its ancestor.

Baptism of one sort or another is common in many communities including Central Asia and Tibet.

Running water which purifies is considered good for birth ceremonies. In Britain it is supposed to be unwise to tell the baby's name before the Christening as fairies or evil spirits might steal it.

Arthur Grimble describes an experience which illustrates the power of a name when he was based on one of the Gilbert Islands in the early 1900s. 'No white baby had ever been seen before on Tarawa. The villagers seemed never tired of looking at Joan's blue eyes and golden hair. One evening a small naked girl in the crowd mustered to gaze around the pram piped aloud "Ai bia aran te tei-n-aire aie!" (I would that this girl-child's name could be my name). I said "What's all the fuss about? Why shouldn't she?" I turned to Olivia: "Of course she may," she said: "What's to stop it if the mother likes it?" There was a shout of pleasure from the audience. The mother, looking her thanks, led her small girl to the side of the pram and, bending over it, addressed our sleeping Joan with a smile of tender courtesy: "Neiko (Woman), I have thrown away the name of this, my girl child, and taken your name for her instead. Your mother says I may. See, here is your name-sister and servant for evermore, Joan of Betio, who shall obey your word in all things."'

(Arthur Grimble from 'A Pattern of Islands')

NAMES AND MEANINGS

Children used often to be named after the place where they were born, or given their parents' surnames, and in America today baby boys are often given the same forename as their father with a 'Junior' tagged on at the end. But many names have meanings of their own, reflecting the pride the parents feel in their baby sons: names that mean 'brave' or 'immortal' in the hopes that the child will carry the characteristics of his name. Many quite different sounding names may have the same meaning, if they originated in different lands from different languages. Here's a selection of names with special meanings which give them an extra charm.

ADAM: *man* or *red earth* (Hebrew)

ADRIAN: *of the Adriatic* (Latin)

ALAN: *little rock* (Celtic)

ALASTAIR, ALASDAIR: Scottish form of Alexander

ALBERT: *noble and bright* (Old English)

ALEXANDER: *helper* or *defender of men*, a name given to Paris in the Iliad for his courage in repelling robbers from the flocks.

ALEXIS: *helper* (Greek and Russian)

ALFRED: *elf counsel* (Old English)
AMBROSE: *immortal* (Greek)
ANDREW: *a man* (Greek)
ANGUS: *unique choice* (Gaelic, Irish and Scottish)
ARCHIBALD: *true and bold* (Germanic)
ARTHUR: *bear* (Celtic from Indo-Europe)

BARRY: *spearlike* or *spearman* (Irish)
BASIL: *kingly* (Greek)
BENEDICT: *blessed* (Latin)
BENJAMIN: *son of the right hand* (Hebrew)
BRUNO: *brown* or *bright* (Germanic)

CASPER: *horseman* (Persian—also traditional name
      for one of the Three Kings)
CHARLES: *freeman* (Old High German)
CHRISTIAN: *follower of Christ* (Latin)
CHRISTOPHER: *he who carried Christ* (St. Christopher
      carried the Christ child and the
      whole world across a river.)
CLEMENT: *merciful* (Latin—the name of fourteen
      popes)
COLIN: *dove* (Latin, though in Scotland it may come
      from the French pet form of Nicholas)

CONOR: *high will* or *high courage* (Irish)
CONRAD: *bold counsel* (Germanic)
CURTIS: *courteous* (US, derived from Old French)
CYRIL: *lordly* (Greek)

DAMIAN: *one who tames* (Greek)
DANIEL: *God has judged* (Hebrew)
DAVID: *beloved* (Hebrew)
DOMINIC: *of the Lord* (it often means 'Child born on Sunday')
DONALD: *world* and *rule* (Celtic)
DOUGLAS: *dark blue* (originally Celtic river name, then Scottish clan name)
DYLAN: *sea* (Welsh)
DUNCAN: *brown* and *battle* (Celtic)
DUNSTAN: *hill* and *stone* (Old English)

EDGAR: *prosperous spear* (Old English)
EDWARD: *treasure* and *guardian* (Old English)
ENOCH: *dedicated* (Hebrew)
ERIC: *forever* and *power* (Old Norse)
ESMOND: *grace + protection* (Irish, probably from Old English)

EUGENE: *well born* (Greek)
EVAN: *young warrior* (Celtic, also Welsh form of John)
EVELYN: *pleasant* (Celtic)

FELIX: *happy* (Latin)
FERDINAND: *voyaging, venturer* (Germanic)
FRANCIS: *Frenchman* (Germanic)
FREDERICK: *peaceful ruler* (Latin)

GABRIEL: *man of god* (Hebrew)
GAVIN: *from Sir Gawain, one of King Arthur's knights*
GEORGE: *earthworker or husbandman* (Greek)
GERALD: *spear thrower* (Germanic)
GODFREY: *god and peace* (Norman)
GREGORY: *a watchman* (Greek)

HAROLD: *ruler of an army* (Old English)
HARVEY: *warrior* (Germanic or Celtic)

HECTOR: *holding fast* (Greek)
HENRY: *home ruler* (Old High German)
HEW, HUGH: *mind* (presumably intellect, from Celtic)
HILARY: *cheerful* (Latin)
HUBERT: *clever* (Germanic)
HUGH: *heart, mind, spirit* (Norman)
HUMPHREY: *peaceful giant* (Old High German)

IDRIS: *battle king* (Welsh)
ISAAC: *laughter* (Hebrew)

KEITH: *wood* (Gaelic)
KENNETH: *handsome* (Celtic)
KIEREN: *black* (Celtic)

LEO: *lion* (Greek)
LLOYD: *grey* (Welsh)

MAGNUS: *great* (Scandinavian)
MARTIN: from Mars—Roman god of war

MATTHEW: *gift of Jehova* (Hebrew)
MAURICE: *moor* (Latin)
MICHAEL: *who is like God* (Hebrew)
MILES: *servant of Mary* (either Old French or Irish)
MONTAGUE: *a peaked hill* (French)
MORGAN: *sea dweller* (Welsh)
MUNGO: *lovable* (Gaelic)

NATHAN: *a gift* (Hebrew)
NEAL: *a champion* (Irish)
NOAH: *rest* (Hebrew)

OTTO: *rich* (German)
OWEN: *young warrior* (Welsh)

PATRICK: *nobleman* (Latin)
PAUL: *small* (Latin)
PEREGRINE: *wanderer* (Latin)
PETER: *stone* (Greek)
PHILIP: *fond of horses* (Greek)
PROSPER: *lucky* (Latin)

R

RICHARD: *a hard ruler* (Old French)
REX: *king* (Latin)
ROBERT: *stardom* (Old French)
RODERICK: *famous ruler* (Old High German)
ROGER: *fame and spear* (German)
RORY: *red* (Irish)
RUSSELL: *red head* (Old French)

S

SAMPSON: *child of the sun* (Hebrew)
SEBASTIAN: *venerable* (Latin)
SEPTIMUS: *the seventh* (Latin)
SILVESTER: *belonging to a forest* (Latin)
SIMEON: *obedient, harkening* (Hebrew)
SIMON: *snub nosed* (Greek)
STEPHEN: *a garland* (Greek)

T

THEODORE: *God's gift* (Greek)
THOMAS: *twin* (Greek)
TIMOTHY: *honour God* (Greek)

VALENTINE: *strong* (Latin)
VINCENT: *conquering* (Latin)
VIVIAN: *alive* (Latin)

WALDO: *to rule* (Old High German)
WILLIAM: *resolution* (Old German)

FATHER AND SON

'Dombey was about eight-and-forty years of age. Son about eight-and-forty minutes. Dombey was rather bald, rather red, and though a handsome, well-made man, too stern and pompous in appearance, to be prepossessing. Son was very bald, and very red and though (of course) an undeniably fine infant, somewhat crushed and spotty in his general effect, as yet. On the brow of Dombey, Time and his brother Care had set some marks, as on a tree that was to come down in good time—forests, notching as they go—while the countenance of Son was crossed and recrossed with a thousand little creases, which the same deceitful Time would take delight in smoothing out and wearing away with the flat part of his scythe, as a preparation of the surface for his deeper operations.'

(Charles Dickens from
Dombey and Son)

GERMAN LULLABY

Sleep, little one, and be good,
The birds are all in the wood:
They fly in the wood
From tree to tree,
And soon they will bring
Sweet sleep to thee.
Eia, eia, poppeia!